Crayola

LET'S DRAW MONSTERS WITH CRAYOLA!

ILLUSTRATED BY SUSANNA RUMIZ

LERNER PUBLICATIONS MINNEAPOLIS

© 2018 Crayola, Easton, PA 18044-0431. Crayola Oval Logo, Crayola, Serpentine Design, Pink Flamingo, Carnation Pink, Vivid Tangerine, Unmellow Yellow, Mountain Meadow, and Blue Bell are registered trademarks of Crayola used under license.

Official Licensed Product
Lerner Publications Company
A division of Lerner Publishing Group, Inc.
241 First Avenue North
Minneapolis, MN 55401 USA

For reading levels and more information, look up this title at www.lernerbooks.com.

Main body text set in Billy Infant Regular 24/30.
Typeface provided by SparkyType.

Library of Congress Cataloging-in-Publication Data

Names: Rumiz, Susanna, illustrator.
Title: Let's Draw Monsters with Crayola®! / illustrated by Susanna Rumiz.
Description: Minneapolis : Lerner Publications, 2018. | Series: Let's Draw with Crayola®! | Includes bibliographical references. | Audience: Ages 4-9. | Audience: K to Grade 3. | Includes bibliographical references. | Description based on print version record and CIP data provided by publisher; resource not viewed.
Identifiers: LCCN 2017009634 (print) | LCCN 2017018541 (ebook) | ISBN 9781512497779 (eb pdf) | ISBN 9781512432947 (lb : alk. paper)
Subjects: LCSH: Monsters in art—Juvenile literature. | Drawing—Technique—Juvenile literature.
Classification: LCC NC825.M6 (ebook) | LCC NC825.M6 D73 2018 (print) | DDC 743.6—dc23

LC record available at https://lccn.loc.gov/2017009634

Manufactured in the United States of America
1-41825-23785-7/20/2017

CONTENTS

Can You Draw a Monster?........ 4

One-Eyed Monsters 6

Toothy Monsters 8

Monster Faces 10

Furry Monsters 12

Multi-Limbed Monsters 14

Multi-Eyed Monsters 16

Water Monsters 18

Undead Monsters 20

Flying Monsters 22

Tentacle Monsters 24

Scaly Monsters 26

Monster Barbecue 28

World of Colors..................... 30
To Learn More 32

CAN YOU DRAW A MONSTER?

You can if you can draw shapes! Follow the steps and use the shapes to draw furry monsters, scaly monsters, flying monsters, and more. Or create your own monster!

MONSTER BASICS

Shapes you will use: oval square triangle circle rectangle half circle

Chompers

Eyes

Manes and Scales

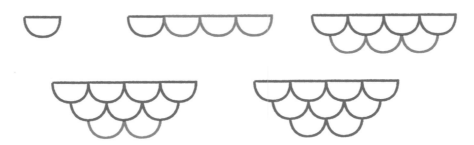

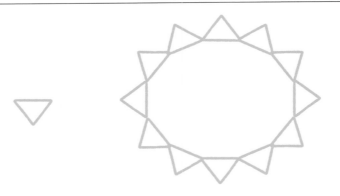

Paws and Claws

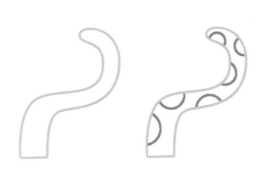

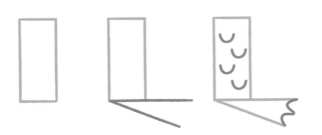

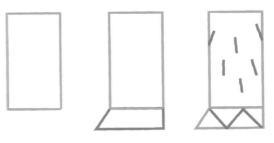

ONE-EYED MONSTERS

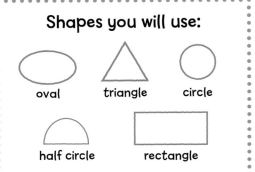

Shapes you will use:

oval   triangle   circle

half circle   rectangle

One-Eyed Frilled Lizard Monster

iCat

6

Swamp Eye

Cyclops Susan

7

TOOTHY MONSTERS

Fang

Smiley

8

Tri-Tooth

Chomper

GRRR

9

MONSTER FACES

RRRibbit

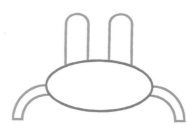

PRRR

Blobalong

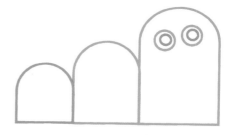

10

Frank

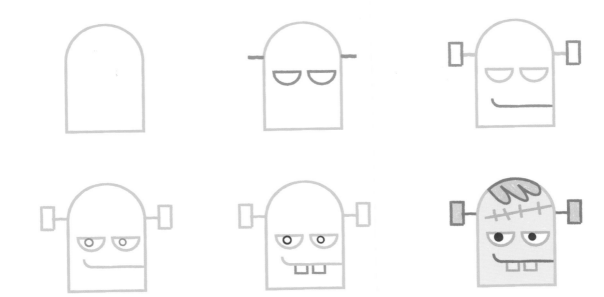

Toasty

FURRY MONSTERS

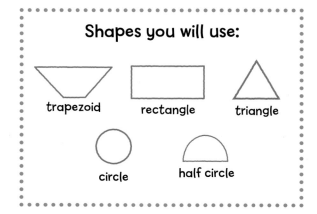
Harry

Fuzzy Fred

Shaggy

13

MULTI-LIMBED MONSTERS

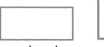
Hot Shot

14

Dine-o-Monster

MULTI-EYED MONSTERS

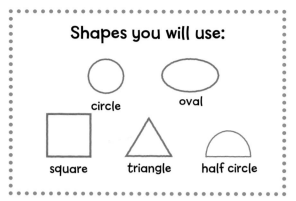
Three Eyes

16

Bullseye

Spied-Her

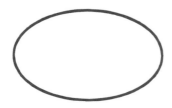 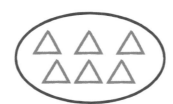 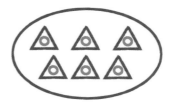

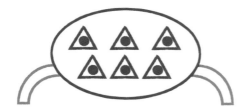 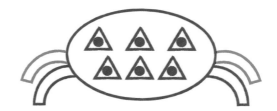

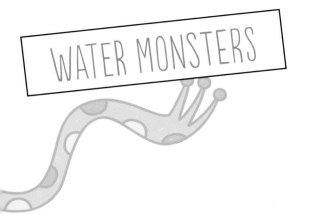

WATER MONSTERS

Patchy

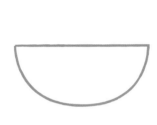

Jelly

Bubbles

19

Undead Fred

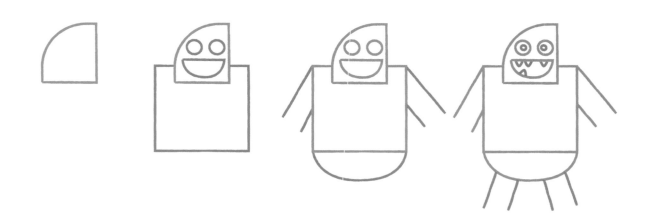

Music Mummy

Boneshaker

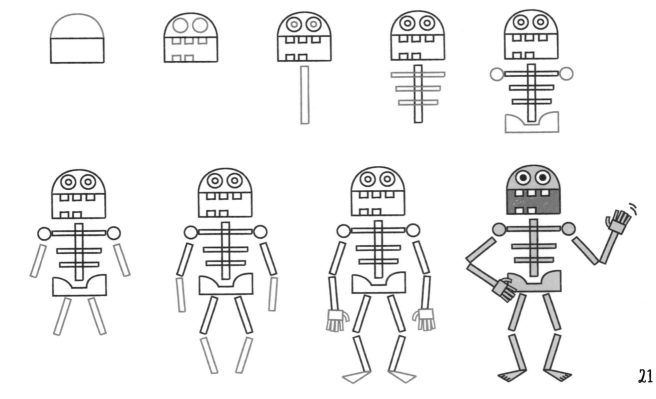

21

FLYING MONSTERS

Wingsy

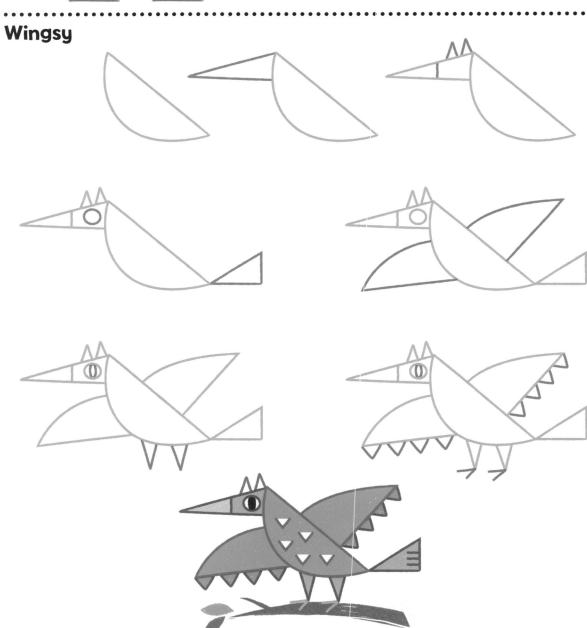

Yorick

TENTACLE MONSTERS

Shapes you will use:

 circle half circle triangle oval

Roller

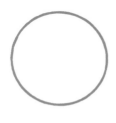

Jeeves

SCALY MONSTERS

Coolasaurus

Tiny Dancer

Monstrich

27

WORLD OF COLORS

Colors are everywhere—even in the monster world! Here are some of the Crayola® crayon colors used in this book. What colors will you use to draw your next monster?

RED

PINK FLAMINGO

CARNATION PINK

SALMON

RED ORANGE

VIVID TANGERINE

SUNGLOW

UNMELLOW YELLOW

CANARY

ArRRGH! DRAWING IS FUN!

GREEN YELLOW

SEA GREEN

YELLOW GREEN

MOUNTAIN MEADOW

GREEN

SKY BLUE

TURQUOISE BLUE

AQUAMARINE

BLUE BELL

GRAY

Crayola®

TO LEARN MORE

Books

Bergin, Mark. *It's Fun to Draw Monsters.* New York: Skyhorse, 2013.
Follow the step-by-step instructions in this book to learn how to draw more monsters.

Garbot, Dave. *Mean 'n' Messy Monsters.* Irvine, CA: Walter Foster, 2015.
Learn how to draw your favorite monsters in cartoon form in this fun book.

StJohn, Amanda. *5 Steps to Drawing Monsters.* Mankato, MN: Child's World, 2012.
Read fun facts about monsters before you learn to draw classic monsters in this book.

Websites

Draw a Monster
http://artprojectsforkids.org/draw-a-monster/
Turn your monster drawings into art! Visit this website to learn how to create pieces of art using your monster drawing skills.

My Monster Power Cards
http://www.crayola.com/crafts/my-monster-power-cards-craft/
Create power cards for your favorite monsters, and add information about their special powers and skills. What powers will your monsters have?